THE INHABITED INITIAL

For Doug, Susie and Ursula.

As always.

THE INHABITED INITIAL

Fiona Farrell

drawings by Ann Culy

AUCKLAND UNIVERSITY PRESS

First published 1999

Auckland University Press
University of Auckland
Private Bag 92019
Auckland
New Zealand
http://www.auckland.ac.nz/aup

© Fiona Farrell, 1999
© Ann Culy, 1999 (drawings)

ISBN 1 86940 215 4

Publication is assisted by

Illustrations by Ann Culy
Design by Karina McLeod
Printed through Planet Media, Wellington

Contents

To the point

The origin of the exclamation mark was the Latin word "Io",
meaning "Hurrah!", which was inserted into manuscripts
by medieval scribes.

The question mark is a "Q" above an "o", an abbreviation
for "quaestio", the Latin word for "an enquiry".

The full stop was inserted into continuous lines of
text by Roman scribes.

Punctuation

Each line a hollow stem
filled with meaning.
Each dot an egg-sac
squirming, each squiggle
setting root where it falls.
The membrane on each
mark vibrating to the beat
(ta dum ta dum)
of heart and wings.

!!!

Exclamation mark

Click. Click.

A woman writes
in a quiet room.

There are others
writing with their
heads lowered,
their faces hidden.

Click. Click.

It might be the
crack of ivory on
wood, the snapping
of human bone bent
to the image of god.

Click. Click.

She smiles, demure
beneath her wimple.
She is writing joy!
She is writing a line
in flight above the sun.
She is writing the
one-legged man of the
joke, leaping to the

3

punchline. She is
over in the corner writing
ecstasy and the clicking
is the sound of her heels
meeting in mid-air.

Io! Io! Io!

? ?

Question mark

Why? asks the earnest enquirer.
How? Who? He marks the question
with a rising inflection. He writes it
as a swan curled over the silent circle of
a lake. It is early morning. It is the time
to ask questions. Why? How? Who?

....

Full stop

The little dot raises its hand.
It breaks into the letters marching
from left to right and forces them to
form cohorts of meaning. It insists
on quiet. Take a breath, it says.
Take it easy.

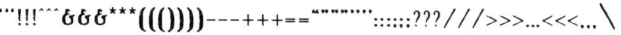

To the point

Not a mark is without meaning.

As night falls we walk
in silence by the sea,
me easy with you,
you easy with me.

Among dry kelp and empty shells
our bare feet print wet sand,
till here, at the end of a tangled
line, we begin to understand.

From the point we look back
and in those marks on the beach
between rock and water
we read the patterns of our speech.

Words, war and water

For the past three months, Dr Zenad has been monitoring the birth defects in their delivery room, where 20 to 30 babies are born daily . . . "August – we had three babies born with no head. Four had abnormally large heads. In September we had six with no heads, none with large heads and two with short limbs. In October, one with no head, four with big heads and four with deformed limbs or other types of deformities . . ."

The most likely origin of this gene-twisting force is not Iraqi but Western. During the 100-hour ground war of February 1991, coalition planes fired at least 1 million rounds of ammunition coated in radio-active material known as depleted uranium, or DU . . . the heaviest metal in the world . . . so tough that bullets coated in DU can slice through tanks like a knife through butter . . .

(Report by Maggie O'Kane in the *Guardian*, January 1999)

nu BREAD-an e-iz-za-at-te-ni
wa-a-tar-ma e-ku-ut-te-ni

Now bread you eat.
Water then you drink.

(This proverb dating from c.2000BC provided a vital
clue to the translation of Hittite.)

1. The translator

The translator dangles
by a thread above
thickets of sound.

He presses his hand at
the small sharp print
of an ancient tongue.

His fingers feel for the
crack where words can
spill from the rock like water.

He seeks it in the boasting
of Azitawadd, bow-legged
King of the Danunites,
whose shaggy men harvested
this place, mowing the
people who grew here
like flowers by a river.
He, Azitawadd, cut them

with his curved sword and
had his scribes write it on
rock. His scribes dangled
by a thread above thickets
of sound: the weeping of
children, the ululation of
a thousand thousand tongues

split to make a human noise.

2. The speech of cups

The translator found more
words in a catalogue.

This was the word for
the two-handled cup,
this the word for the
cup with three handles.

The language peeled back
like a layer of grass.

Like grass cut in straight
lines so it lifts away whole.

And under the grass lay a
whole people, speaking.

They babbled law and love.
The babbled the boasts of
bow-legged potentates and
hymns to the goddess with
her hands full of snakes.
They babbled the story of
the man nailed in a box
adrift on deep water.

Their words left their mouths
like dragon-flies, blue-winged.

Their words spoke from the earth.
They said: this is the word for the
two-handled cup. This is the word
for the cup with three handles.

This is the speech of the trader in cups.

3. The first person

The translator made note of
the little man who knelt and
pointed to his mouth. He
deduced that this must be
the sign for ME. This must
be the first person.

I, Azitawadd, King of the Danunites.

Understand the little man
and the rocks speak. They
dribble words bright as
bubbles. Language flies
from the crack like
dragon-flies, blue-winged.

The little man kneels on
white linen. His hair is
scented with myrrh. He has
a mouth. He has fingers.

This is ME, he says. I
speak. Therefore I must
come first in the sentence.

4. Descartes and the dog

But if you cannot speak, what then?
If you have a tongue, but one fit
only for licking a bowl or drooling
on a hot day, what then?

If your sign is DOG, what then?

The philosopher would have you nailed
to a board to prove his point, a sharp
word driven through each paw.

He would observe that your cry, having
neither syllable nor structure, means
nothing. Yet on any battlefield as the
guns quieten, this is the sound you

hear: the howling of automata, then the
squeaking speech of silence.

5. Hamed Ameri's skull won't stop growing

(   )
(   )
This is the language of war.
Can you hear it?
Not trumpets or drums nor the
thrumming of machines nor the
thud of the big guns. Not the
soldier crooning to his sweetie
as he polishes his boots.
(   )
(   )
This is the sound a child makes
who is born with no head. This
is the sound a woman makes who
labours to bear a child without

mouth, without ears, without
fingers, a child whose head
swells like a pumpkin.

(   )
(   )

Can you hear it?
This is the sound of bone cells
in frenzy. This is the sound of
an eyeball rolling like bruised
fruit in the socket.

(   )
(   )

This is the sound the child hears
who has no ears. This is the sound
of war. This is the blaring of
trumpets and the clapping of
satisfied shareholders. This is the
whistling of the scientist in his
laboratory. This is the babble of
many tongues as they are
simultaneously translated in the

glass towers in the stone city.
This is the burping of fat men
and the scratching of their pens
signatory to all conventions.

(   )
(   )

Can you hear it?
The soft rush of water as the
babies slip onto the table,
crying though they have no mouths
listening though they have no ears
their tendril fingers twisted in
threads of meaning.

6. Terra incognita

When we step ashore from our stinking craft
onto the dazzling sands of terra incognita
we find them waiting: those children whose
heads do grow beneath their shoulders, the

women with the feet of birds, the men who
eat their young.

They emerge, shy, from among trees we have
yet to name. They hand us strange fruits, and
we would eat – but this is a place where our
dreams have come true and in the dream, the
snake speaks and our craft, that encrusted
hulk out there in the blue water, cuts adrift
and leaves us here

squeaking in paradise.

7. Wa-a-tar

Stutter once, and there's the
same water speaking volumes
between willow branches.

It leaves the same mark on a
cracked hand, repeats itself

in the perfect circles of cups
scooped from red clay.

Stutter once, and it dribbles
its familiar cool line from
lip to belly. It breaks out of
darkness at those places where
rock stammers
and becomes uncertain.

Wa-a-tar, said the army breaking
from a dry pass and seeing the
ocean wedged blue between hills.

Wa-a-tar, as they lay at the
margins of a river, supping to the
babble of dry reeds.

Wa-a-tar, to the woman at the well,
one hip jutting to hold the curve of
a jar, the other holding her baby.

Hold out your cup. Hold out your hand,
cracked palm uppermost, and she would
pour you such a quantity of longing.

Such pure beauty.

Wa-a-tar.

Stutter once and we are there:
one of the king's daughters,
walking home among dragonflies
bearing life in both arms.

8. The proverb

I am.
I love.
I sing.
I think.
Now bread you eat.
Water then you drink.

I stand.

I dance.

I fly.

I sink.

Now bread you eat.

Water then you drink.

I breathe.

I speak.

I see.

I blink.

Now bread you eat.

Water then you drink.

I am a flower by the river.

I walk among dragonflies.

I am mother to the big-headed child.

I am the king's daughter.

I eat bread, as you do.

Then I drink water.

New feathers

Through the eyes [we] receive an emanation of beauty . . . and as the nourishing moisture falls upon the soul the roots of each feather under the surface of the soul swell and push upwards. In this, the soul begins to regain it its original state when it was covered with feathers . . .

Socrates (Plato's *Phaedrus*)

Creed

I believe in
the gingerbread man.
Who wouldn't run,
given the circumstances?

But not the Father,
not the Son.

I believe in
forgiveness.

But not in sin.

I believe in
communion: bread wine
apples and us all
happy at table.

But not in saints.

I believe in
life. You have to,
don't you, being alive?

But not everlasting.

Those immortelles, petals
fallen like yellow teeth
in the tomb, bearing the
form of flowers.

But not the scent,
not the breath.

Garden dreams

Turnips

*To dream of a turnip means for the
man that has seen it a matter that is
past and gone so that there is no going
back to it.*

She dreamed that night of turnips.
Their bald white crowns beneath
red earth, their plumes of ragged
green. She dreamed they stretched
and shouldered their way up into
light where they formed ranks and
fought as soldiers do, bleeding
onto desert sand. But that's a
turnip dream. All passed and run to
seed, the soldiers gone to bone in
the far corner of some rumpled sheet.

Saucepans

The sight of a saucepan announces
the conclusion of affairs in
which one is engaged.

She dreamed of a saucepan and
knew that good would come of it.
He'd gather her like a cauliflower
she'd take him like a carrot
and they'd stir all night to
the hiss of a lamp held
upright on her white foot.

Ostriches

The appearance of ostriches is the
prognostication of bad fortune,
news of death, news of peril.

To dream of ostriches is
to dream bad luck. But
to dream of fruit trees is

to dream of daughters
who speak with the voices
of leaves. To dream of the
sea is to dream of the sea.
To dream of a dream is to
dream a horse which enters
a dream about a house
where the dreamer rides
down and down an endless
flight of white birds.

(References to *The Perfumed Garden* by Sheik Nefzaoui, trans. Burton)

First up

I know it's just hormonal a
minute chemical concatenation
ephemeral, pituitary, excess of
oestrogen or some damn
measurable thing. But today
it's spring and bugger glands.
I can see clear to Wharite and
the whole line of hills each
tree each leaf the TV mast
pulsing and someone better
adjust my vertical hold or
I'll roll right off the screen.

*

I love you touselled sleeping
and our children turning and
turning under feathers and
downstairs the budgies
nattering. The plain pattern
of such mornings.

*

They just leave their sneakers
where they've stood stretched
at foot and ankle and their
socks inside. Behind the sofa
jeans curl shed skins and
knickers stained and holding
still their sweet smells. Now
the girls mould sheet and blanket
round their fresh bodies. Like
apples. Like green plums.

*

This morning the birds are
expressing territoriality in
baroque terms. They trill
aggression and ornament
desire. Excess in all things.
They know the score.

Aerogramme

At this distance you
slip into focus. Close
up it's clutter fore
ground fuss and have
you put the bottles
out and have you paid
the gas? Now you slip
each week on a blue
square into the box
an edited version
but yourself clearly.
Between us drifts
infinity this wide air
where planes dwindle
doodling vapour but
in the scribble I can
see you. I can see you.

Fairytale

(For Jane and Antoinette)

There were two sisters in the story.
Remember? One dark, one fair. And a
bear who came in to lie by the fire.
So they learned early that appearances
deceive and that it's wise to be polite
to hags and goblins. Kiss the frogs.
You just can't tell in forests where
light flickers and reality can change
in seconds. And one night the dark
sister walked out and met death who
wasn't old as they expected: dim and
toothless, dwindling to decay but a
young man riding who gathered her up
wild into the storm. And the fair one
seeks her still in daffodils and all
bright vivid things because she knows

that in this forest shapes shift, fit on
new skins, but nothing vanishes
completely. The right words said with
love can spring a sudden transformation.

So she lives. We hope happily.
And we hope ever after.

What it's like

Well, it's kind of like
you're hanging over a
steep drop, fingers
cracking on some old
root or other and below
there's sand or river,
boulders worn to solid
spheres, and you say to
yourself, "Now, I could
let go." And what do
you know?

You do.

And then, it's kind of like
singing with your feet off
the pedals, bush lining a
damp black road downhill
to the corner and a creek

like a crowd hanging about
in dappled shade for you
to whistle by.

And then, it's kind of like
lying on a hillside, sun
full on and a gum tree
rattling away like streamers,
and there's a whole kind of
shining party going on,
and you're at it.

Extras

Third row from the back, she's
beneath the beam watching a
version of events which turns
it all to treachery and love
lost between heroes. One grand
man shot, another betrayed in
a mirrored room. But she is
watching the glass for the
laughing girl who has slipped
out of character, for the dog
pissing, for tyre tracks in the desert,
the descending boom.

Earth

There were stars like these
at the Savoy where we sat
hands chocolate smear
waiting for the main feature
when the curtains rippled
skyward and Tammy was in love.

I lie on wet grass, belly heaving
(the olives probably, or the meat —
some violent intestinal flux) while
overhead the stars rip about
losing it completely. In the dark
I shit and vomit. I smear. I moan.

Then, your hand strokes my forehead.
Your fingers touch my hair. My
darling, you say. My darling.

Of course. You are accustomed to
sick creatures. Cows, pigs and
sheep. You muck me out. You
tuck me in.

And the sky rolls back from the hills
and here it is: the main feature. I
spit into a bowl and I love you.

Deep as dirt.
Clean as grass.
Sure as shit.

Moo, I say.
Moo moo.
Baa.
Oink.

Otanerito

1. Bird

Filaments of light
stretched over the
flex of sea and stone.
Bird at the web
scratch scratch
with red legs.

2. Cliff

Cliff meets sea.
Sea bash at
knuckle rock.
Thump, says sea.
Cliff says
stop.

Fog

These are the names for fog:
the undecided
the deceiver
gauze, as in the trimming of a hat
ribbon, as in the binding of muscle
pillow, at the green mouths of trees
sheet, spread clean over ruin
curtain, drawn up on the old battle

light versus dark
gully versus hilltop.

The functions of fog are:
to lick
to titillate
to withold information
to bring us stumbling to a place
where trees embrace
where men strike at stones

thinking them to be the enemy
where air curdles to the
breathing of thin women
waiting for the bones of
drowned lovers to flick in
on a rising tide.

Two café songs

1. Faux pas in a café

chit chat chit chatter take your order?
chatter chat rattle chat clatter chat
giggle guzzle chat flirt giggle gobble
chat gabble chit chat blurt blurt
blubber blubber bitter shatter wossa
matter? bubble pop rattle rattle
chatter
clatter
rattle
chatter
chit
chat
chit
chit
chat
oh
shit.

2. Politics in a piano bar

Sbeena
goonigh.
Jenny lice a
cigar inna
piannoba
slowman playsa
byebye song
time ago home.
Jonsez molly
nashill bussards
fucka cunry up
carn trussa
bussards like
marxnveeba say eh?
Jenny lice anutha
cigar sez marxis
crap Ima raggill
lesbeen capliss.
drivea lacemodill Jag.

Baman flixis rag.
Jonsez millclass
bitchis carn stan
millclass bitchis.
Jenny puffa poppyglo
inna dark sez gestuff.
An me? Wanna slee
wannago byebye song.

Hard knocks

1. The proposition

The proposition is that
this is alienation that
one kid or can topped u
p and graded labelled p
assed inspection and ro
lling off the line beco
mes like any other that
days converge clock in b
ell class bell tea bell
class bell staff farewe
ll bell class class bel
l clock out. I'm a ligh
t industrial operator f
aced with 30 learning i
nput centres and all al
ong the corridor you ca
n hear the machine at f

ull throttle one hour e
nglish one hour science
maths a run and back fo
r typing. Here Jesus ha
s 40 minutes for the se
rmon on the mount (allo
wing time for questions
) Einstein's got to fit
in relativity and Socra
tes clearly needs to de
fine his objectives. It
's not good the way he
leaves his room and wal
ks round the field, tal
king. Just talking.

2. Glue

They're sniffing glue a
gain on the rough groun
d behind the playing fi

elds. The duty patrol h
as found their bags fla
yed skins tangled in go
rse and fennel and the s
mooth places where they
have lain snug in clay s
nuffing up omnipotence.

So another battle's los
t and won and after lun
ch they tumble back bug
-eyed and giggling brai
n cells popping like li
ght bulbs to learn how
to compose a more Form
al Letter to the Editor.

3. From Room 31 you can see Ruapehu

The mountain is a white
triangle in the upper l

eft hand corner only a
detail on the wider can
vas which is as always
concrete brick and fart
ing humanity but it's t
he bit that matters bec
ause on a clear morning
4T at your back gagging
on facts turned in turn
ed off and turned on, w
ell, it's there isn't i
t? One hard and pure pe
rfect thing. Ice rock a
nd fire drawing the eye.

4. Statistical survey

Approximately 40% of m
aori girls between 15 an
d 20 don't have jobs an

d approximately 25% of

maori boys and if you'r

e pakeha the chances ar

e 1 in 7 not good odds

either but approximatel

y 90% of politicians th

ink they'll do and here

approximately 94 units

on the demograph are bei

ng taught something app

roximating literature b

y someone who is approx

imately me and Lee has b

een absent 32 half days

this term and has a rea

ding age of 8 and Dean

has an IQ of 102 and 4

minor convictions and R

osa with her broken eye

s is 3 months gone and

if a thousand thousand n

umbers are planted 1 m
etre apart in regular s
urveys, how many numb
ers will it take to fill a
country's cup, approxim
ately?

5. Instructions for play

Here's a word: stone. H
ard. Snug in the hand.
Throw it well.

Here's a word: scissors
. Sharp. For cutting ta
pe, thick skins. Be care
ful, but not too carefu
l. Direct the point awa
y from your own young
body. Here's a word: pap
er. Flares in a second,

lifts off into the dark
shedding sparks above t
he heads of the people,
yet a child can smooth
it, cool and clear, and
fold it to make a bird
which really flies on r
eal wings.

Beside myself

Oh I do like to be beside this
sea she's giddy kicks her heels
drops her knickers at my feet
white frills. And further out
pom pom she shows seams on
sheer silk and little tumbling
shells. The hills stand back
black hair slicked flat baring
their chests and a whole brass
band of gulls and tiddly dotterels
reels past screech. I'm too old to
do cart-wheels at the beach (I'm
the one in the woolly hat walking
by the water) but inside, I'm turning

over

and

over

and

over.

Sheep

Last week, they stood about the paddock
solid as a chesterfield suite. They
moved slowly, their black feet concealed
beneath the fleece. They took seriously
this business of eat and sleep, teaching
their lambs to chew slowly, to conduct
themselves as sheep. On Saturday, the
truck came, rattled down the road, and
the lambs were taken. Oh, heavy load!
They cried, the mothers. How they grieved,
calling all night to the dark hills.
Where are you, my sweet-scented darling?
Where are you, whom I licked one slick
green day from bloody ground? The valley
echoed with the sound of lamentation.
But today, they have forgotten. They have
been shorn and, stripped in an instant, they
leap free, creatures new-born. There is no

hill too steep, no creek they cannot cross.
Light enough to leap fences, and a whole
lifetime before it starts again:

the loving and the loss.

Ursula at Parakakariki

My white bird stands
by a southern sea,
arms lifted wide
to fly from me.

Once, she stood on my hand
fingers caught in my hair.
Now she steps from land
to thin bright air.

From earth scraped red-raw
and seeded with bone
she rises in feathers,
she flies alone.

At the fine wire
between day and night
she flies feathered in soft rain,
feathered in light.

'But where's this country's soul?'
asked the visiting novelist . . .

It is written in the bird code
of the old philosophers.

It is in the curl of a fist
unfurling like bracken shoot.

It is in my cousin's jersey.
My aunt wrote that jersey
in purl and plain, using
nothing but a pair of pointed
sticks.

It is in block letters at dam or bridge
and in the sly graffiti of water at
their foundations.

It is scrawled in dust
with a skid! and a whoop!
at the corners.

It is in the sweet calligraphy of air.

It is passed breath to breath.

It is not always available for comment.

In a nutshell

Two weeks ago she said
she'd get a bike when
summer came, and I
thought her brave and
wild: my own mother-
child. Now, she cannot
stand. Her skins hangs
in folds like heavy linen.
Her hands are shot silk
blue and brown like the
frock she wore for dancing.

*

. . . for you praised Him dancing
with timbrel and harp.
You praised Him dancing
alone in the dark . . .

*

Chrissie is in blue candlewick.
Olive lies flat in white. Miss
Strang wants to go home. All
week above their thistle heads
the ward screen leaps with youth
going for gold. They run and dive
and punch the air. Take that!
Take that! But down here, the air
is punching back.

*

She breathes
one breath
to every
four ticks
on the
ward clock.
The pulse at
her neck beats
five to every
four. Air ripples

at her lips, the
tiny suck of the
tide. A fuzzy moon
rides over the city.

*

*. . . for you danced to the wireless
in an empty room,
light in the arms
of the one true bridegroom . . .*

*

In her house, my sister slams
and I yell, chucking death out.
We are huge with grief, two
fat babies struggling to get a
grip. Do you give in? Do you
give in? And in our fat fists
not one another but some dark
secret thing which will not be
flung to the floor.

*

We arrange our mother like a
flower, dry leaf hands beneath
the quilt, head drooping like a
lily bud on its withered stem.

*

I sing her all the songs and
she walks away in perfect time,
down that long, long trail
through that still dark vale,
heading for the sunny
side by side.

*

*. . . your husband was no dancer.
He stumbled on stone,
lost in the desert
while you danced alone . . .*

*

Her pink mouth gapes, eyes
lidded, the blinds already
drawn. She breathes. And
breathes. She is a bird in a
dry land. I dab at her lips
with water on a cotton bud.
She is a bird under a brilliant
sun. She tongues the water,
drop by bitter drop.

*

She perches on my smallest
finger. She lifts her dry mouth
and sings her gurgling song.
It is always for her just this
early morning. It is always
for her this clear day. And
she is poised for ever at just
this instant of flight.

*

. . . on faded pink Feltex
you danced cheek to cheek
with Jesus, who partners
the poor and the meek . . .

*

Her pulse
pecks,
a chick at
thin shell.

She breathes.

She stops.

*

She was always slipping away. Out
through the gaps between words or
between people. Out through the
holes in the fences we tried to build
around her from love, embarrassment
and pity. Now, she makes herself small,

so small she thinks we'll hardly notice.
She holds her tiny breath and slips away
between our clutching fingers.

*

The tide seeps
from the mudflats.
Our eyes dazzle.
Our eyes water.

*

The first calls her 'Mother'.
'We can view Mother,' he
says, 'in the lounge.'
The second calls her 'Mum'
and he'll throw in the catering
for a little extra. The third calls
her both 'Mum' and 'Mother'
and offers a full range of options.
But for you, I'd have a dance:
a country hall, a band playing

'Mexicali Rose' and sausage rolls
for supper. Not this. Not this.
The floral tribute.
Mid-range casket.
Loved Wife and Mother of . . .

*

*. . . your daughters curled
in the burrows of night,
you danced in your dress
that caught all the light . . .*

*

Each night she tucked us in
to bed, prayers said, so the
world rolled steady through
the dark. 'Roll over,' she'd
say. 'Roll over. Face the wall
and you'll have good dreams.'
And on wet nights, rain in the
spouting seeping, she'd say,

'It's a fine night, good for
sleeping.' Now, she is here:
tucked in, feet to the sea, head
to the hill, yellow Merton clay
drawn up to keep off the chill
and overhead a lark etching its
shining song on the dark as rain
drives in from the south. 'Night
night,' we say, our mouths soft
with weeping. 'It's a fine night,
my darling. A fine night for sleeping.'

*

*... for you praised Him dancing
with timbrel and harp.
You praised Him dancing
alone in the dark ...*

*

Angels at her feet and
angels at her head.

Little bird mouth gaping
tonguing holy bread.

Doll eyes spun to zero.

All things done and said.

My mother in a nutshell.

She lived

and now

she's dead.

All the things U are

U are cup and candle
the perfume of
unguents
poured on warm stone

the
ululation
of birds at cliff edge

the tiny flap of the
uvula
marking the borders of
utterance

the tug of the
umbilicus
life knotted at one end
undulating
like a fine red balloon.

The inhabited initial

These poems are intended as meditations on the miracle of the western
alphabet and its origins in early Semitic pictograms.

aleph: an ox

Boustrophedon

She draws the others after
dees worruf gnol eht nwod
dropped in dark trenches.
reh fo enil eht wollof eW
going to the fence and
.toof yvaeh yb toof kcab.

B

ר

beth: a house

This bivvy shelters all
our gods and treasures.
We huddle reading the
calligraphy of fitful
flame, in our tumbled
dreaming the murmur of
mothers like blood round
the belly and beyond the
open window the grunt and
howl of things we cannot
name.

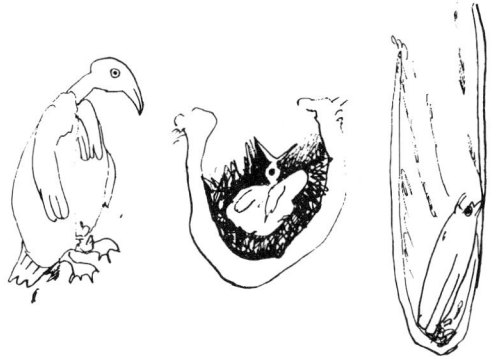

gimel: a camel

It sways toward us sewn in a
secret pocket with strange
seeds and stones. A cup with
a foreign cut carried across
dry land.

daleth: a door

You open it and everything
pours in: new stuff, old
stuff, some for the dump.
You shut it fast, but there's
always some small fist
hammering at the other side.

E

Ǝ

he: lo!

Behold! The Word is striding
high in new shoes! The mark
of its heel is stone. The mark
of its toe is feather and the
skin of unborn lambs. The
Word spans the air-bridge with
curlicue and flourish. Make
straight the way! Make room!
Make a cake!

F

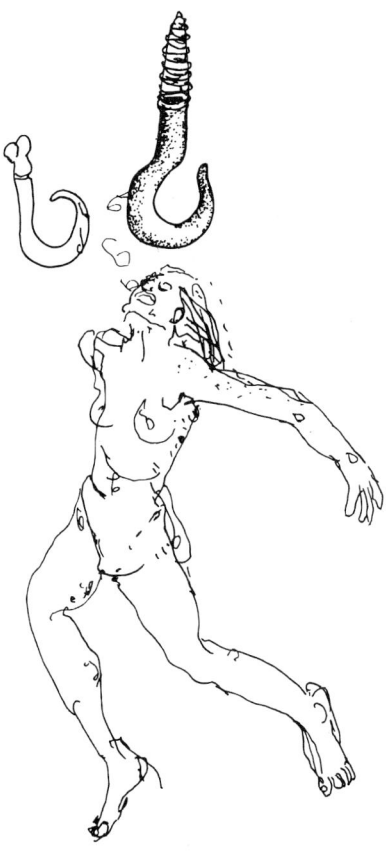

ㅋ

vau: a hook

Meaning hangs like a silk dress,
a heavy coat. There. Behind the
door waiting the structure of a
breathing body to plump and move.

G

gimel: a camel

Here it comes again from
another direction, dust fluff
at each footfall and on to dots
and silence . . .

H

heth: an enclosure

Teeth drawn up, a white pallisade
and through the palings wag woof
and oink moo click suck burp cluck
and yap yap yap yap yap.

I

yod: a hand

Finger or fist. Take that!
Take that! If you would
rule a people, first force
them to eat your words.

J

yod: a hand

On the one hand, chaos.
On the other, order.
And down the middle,
the jagged blast of
knowing.

kap: the palm of the hand

And here's the bird-print of the
goddess, her creatures owl and
hedgehog, bloody as birth and
spiked with sticky jig-a-jig.
She examines the pattern on a
new leaf and says: look, look.
See how the heart cuts across
the other lines.

L

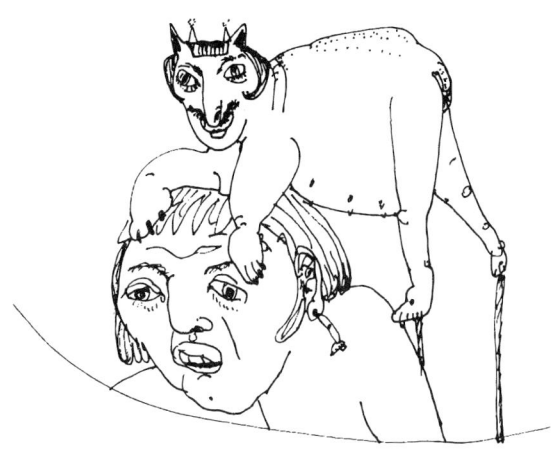

L

lamed: a goad

You gotta move. You gotta
figure it all out. You gotta
go with the babble of brook
and creek and out into the
main current where the flow
is thunder, driving us all to
the edge and over.
Raus! Raus!

mem: water

When a word is launched it
bobs about like a little red
boat under a proper sun on
the blue stripe of now.
Go, little boat. Go.

nun: a snake

This letter wriggles through
dry leaves slipping from skin
to skin.

O

cayin: the eye

I see you. Yes, I see it all
through your round window.
The well, the bubble, the tear.
No pupil. Just your perfect
bowl, holding nothing but
white water.

pe: the mouth

Her mouth a puckered kiss
breath popping like seed
from a dandelion to settle
on other hillsides, other
mouths soft and damp as
flowers, with their roots
down deep.

qoph: a monkey

The tricky ones skip and mimic.

No wonder the bootmen are

burning books, clipping the square

for another winter. But on the

fence above their sweaty heads,

the letters tease. Catch us, bootmen!

Catch us if you can!

9

res: the head

You've got your head screwed
on backwards, looking over
your shoulder. You keep your
head, though, under fire. You
growl. You bare your little teeth.
You say: heads I win, tails I win.
You are strong, backwards or
forwards.

shin: teeth

The word bites, leaving a ragged
edge and a tiny bubble of blood.
It goes off to sit in its box,
tasting memory.

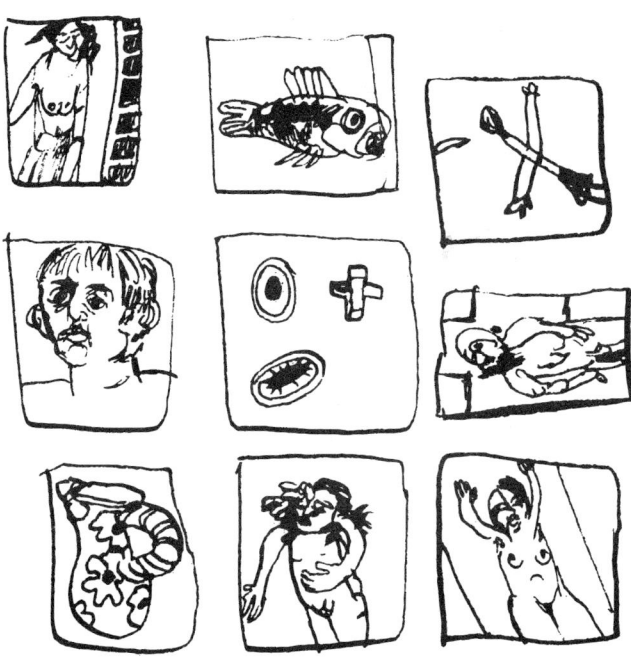

taw: a sign

What signs are these? Crossed sticks,

pointing every way. Grass bent in the

direction of travel. A man whose arms

are spread like a cormorant's wings to

dry in the blast of faith. And down here,

he's 4 her.

In red and black

by the railway track

he sets the old refrain.

I Am

I Love

to the clickety-clack

of every passing train.

ꟻ

vau: a hook

High five!
Up yours!
Come. Go.
Bless. Bash.
Some letters
hang on by
living hand
to mouth.

V

ꓕ

vau: a hook

Snagged in the mouth by a sharp
hook we were lifted to flap about
growing legs on the bank. At brain
stem's root the memory that once
we drew a perfect wake across a
still morning when there was no
sound but air comparing notes with
water.

ך

vau: a hook

Waa waa

baby cry.

Waa waa.

Maa maa.

Daa daa

X

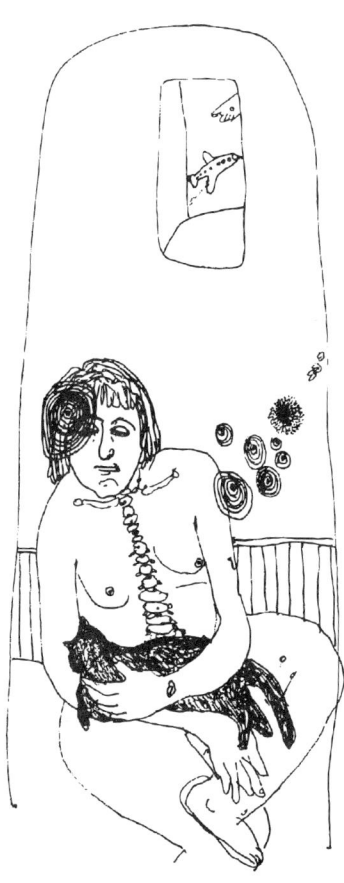

samech: a prop

They hold us straight as a
row of beans. Without them,
we'd flop and muddle. Futharc
and ogam on wooden stakes.
Majuscule, uncial and all those
clever bastards who have spelled
out our rattle and marked the
spot where we were lying,
buried.

Y

ᴴ

v a u : a h o o k

Here it is, shaking above the
hidden spring. And here it is,
split for two wishes. And
here it is, wine flowering on
a slender stem. Break the
glass with a dancing foot.
Let the wine run.

Z

Ⅰ

zayin: lightning

In a flash, all is made plain:
it's an ordinary tale passed
breath to breath, like living.
We perch, claws caught in
the skin of a shining tree.
We sing with our heads
tilted to the storm. We sing
the song that is known only
in this valley. We pass it on.